FREEPORT
MEMORIAL LIBRARY

Presented by

Freeport High School Class
of 1978
30th Class Reunion

2008

"I could never forgive myself if I elected to live without humane purpose, without trying to help the poor and unfortunate, without recognizing that perhaps the purest joy in life comes with trying to help others."

—Arthur Ashe

ARTHUR ASHE: ATHLETE AND ACTIVIST

BY KEVIN CUNNINGHAM

Content Adviser: Tony Lance,
Assistant Editor, Tennis Magazine

The Child's World

Published in the United States of America by The Child's World®
PO Box 326
Chanhassen, MN 55317-0326
800-599-READ
www.childsworld.com

The Child's World®: Mary Berendes, Publishing Director
Editorial Directions, Inc.: E. Russell Primm, Editorial Director; Emily J. Dolbear,
Line Editor; Katie Marsico, Assistant Editor; Matthew Messbarger, Editorial Assistant;
Susan Hindman, Copy Editor; Sarah E. De Capua, Proofreader; Marsha Bonnoit,
Peter Garnham, Terry Johnson, Chris Simms, and Stephan Carl Wender,
Fact Checkers; Tim Griffin/IndexServ, Indexer; Dawn Friedman,
Photo Researcher; Linda S. Koutris, Photo Selector

Cover photograph: Arthur Ashe in 1969 / © Hulton Archive/Getty Images

Interior photographs ©: AP/Wide World Photos: 6, 11, 13, 14, 18, 21, 26, 28; Marty Lederhandler/AP/
Wide World Photos: 17; Michael Lipchitz/AP/Wide World Photos: 30; Lana Harris/AP/Wide World
Photos: 31; Malcolm Clarke/AP/Wide World Photos: 35; Hulton-Deutsch Collection/Corbis: 9, 23;
Bettmann/Corbis: 16, 19, 20, 22, 27; Reuters NewMedia Inc./Corbis: 32, Duomo/Corbis: 36; Hulton
Archive/Getty Images: 2; Gerry Cranham/Time Life/Getty Images: 25; Denis Waugh/Time Life/
Getty Images: 29; Robin Platzer/Time Life/Getty Images: 34; Richmond Times-Dispatch: 8.

Library of Congress Cataloging-in-Publication Data
Cunningham, Kevin (Kevin H.)
Arthur Ashe : athlete and activist / by Kevin Cunningham.
p. cm. — (Journey to freedom)
Includes bibliographical references and index.
ISBN 1-59296-228-9 (lib. bdg. : alk. paper) 1. Ashe, Arthur—Juvenile literature. 2. Tennis players—
United States—Biography—Juvenile literature. 3. Political activists—United States—Juvenile literature.
[1. Ashe, Arthur. 2. Tennis players. 3. African Americans—Biography.] I. Title. II. Series.
GV994.A7C86 2005
796.342'092—dc22   2003027076

Contents

ARTHUR ASHE LEARNED THE IMPORTANCE OF HARD WORK FROM HIS FATHER. ARTHUR ASHE SR., HERE WITH ARTHUR JR. IN 1969, SET HIGH STANDARDS FOR HIS SON.

Learning the Game

Arthur Ashe once said he would consider himself a failure if people remembered him only as a tennis player. By that standard, he was a huge success. At the end of his life, Ashe had achieved fame and accomplished many things as a coach, an author, and an **activist.**

Arthur Ashe Jr. was born on July 10, 1943, in Richmond, Virginia, to Arthur Ashe Sr., a park worker and police officer, and Mattie Cordell Cunningham Ashe. Like all cities in the South at that time, Richmond was **segregated.** Oddly enough, many blacks in Richmond played the traditionally "white" game of tennis. Arthur Jr., skinny and a bit sickly, took up tennis when he was seven.

Tragedy hit his family the same year. Mattie Ashe died at the age of 27 during an operation. Arthur's last memory of his mother was seeing her in a blue corduroy robe watching him eat breakfast. Arthur's father was left to raise Arthur and his younger brother Johnnie alone.

Arthur Sr. was stern but loving. He insisted his sons be educated and well behaved. Above all, he told his sons to protect their reputations. He said they should live by the saying, "A good name is worth more than diamonds and gold."

Arthur Sr. also demanded his sons work hard at whatever they did. He set a good example. When not patrolling the parks, he worked at landscaping or catering. In middle age, he even built a new house out of materials he had gathered himself. His older son took the lessons to heart.

Whites often looked down on blacks in Richmond. Many African-Americans responded to poverty and poor treatment by lashing out. Ashe later remembered the pressure to behave properly. "When some old black lady, maybe your grandmother . . . on her way home from cleaning the white people's houses, saw you or any other black boy doing something wrong, there was one expression she would use that you did not want to hear," he said. "It meant you were letting everybody down—your friends, your family, your history. And that expression was, 'Boy, you should be ashamed of yourself.' Lord, the weight those words carried."

Though small and timid, Ashe showed a gift for tennis. He learned the game from Ron Charity, a part-time coach. Arthur played at an African-American tennis club and at local "black" parks. Despite his talent, officials refused to let him play against whites in the city tournament. Arthur never forgot what it felt like to be refused in that way.

FROM AN EARLY AGE, ARTHUR ASHE TOOK TENNIS SERIOUSLY. HE LEARNED THE GAME ON SEGREGATED TENNIS COURTS.

Arthur aimed high. When he was 13, he told friends he wanted to go to the University of California at Los Angeles (UCLA). His friends laughed—few African-American athletes went to UCLA in those days. And those few played football or basketball, not a country club game like tennis.

Arthur worked with Robert Walter Johnson, a well-known doctor and former tennis player who trained many young blacks. Johnson coached Althea Gibson, who became the first African-American to win Wimbledon and the U.S. National Championships (now called the U.S. Open) in 1957. In 1958, she again won both tournaments.

Arthur began to travel with Johnson to compete against better and better players. Often he was the only African-American in a tournament—when he could get in. Many whites-only tennis clubs had no interest in letting a black player compete. Those that did often wouldn't let him use their locker room.

LIKE ARTHUR ASHE, ALTHEA GIBSON, HERE IN 1956, WORKED WITH TENNIS COACH ROBERT WALTER JOHNSON. A PIONEER IN SPORTS, GIBSON DIED IN 2003.

To add to the pressure, Johnson did not allow Arthur to show his emotions, no matter how frustrated he became. As an adult, Ashe recalled Johnson's words: " 'Don't give anybody the slightest reason to throw you out.' He told me I'd be cheated on line calls—and I was—but to never complain. Just play the points, and keep everything inside." Arthur developed a cool self-control that would later make him famous. It was a hard lesson. "I envied players who could sling a racket and get away with it," he said.

Arthur began to play in tournaments for teenagers (called juniors). He soon earned a reputation as an up-and-coming player. Fans commented on his mental toughness. He seemed always to bounce back.

Life off the court was often tougher. When he was 15, Arthur played in a tournament in Charlottesville, Virginia. That night, he went with a group of white players to the movies. When the theater turned out to be for whites only, he had to stay outside.

During a trip to a major juniors tournament in Kalamazoo, Michigan, Arthur won over crowds with his risk-taking style of tennis. At night, tournament officials threw a dance. Most African-American players stayed away, but Arthur went. Though still quiet and thoughtful, Arthur was beginning to leave the timid Richmond boy behind. As one of his friends put it, "He felt he belonged, and that's what it takes."

ARTHUR ASHE (RIGHT) AND HIS DOUBLES PARTNER SHAKE HANDS WITH THEIR OPPONENTS AT A JUNIORS TOURNAMENT IN 1959. BEING BLACK IN A SPORT TRADITIONALLY FOR WHITE PLAYERS WAS A CONSTANT CHALLENGE.

Inside the White Lines

Arthur Ashe spent his senior year of high school in St. Louis, Missouri. He lived and trained with a black tennis coach named Richard Hudlin. Most of the best tournaments for teen players were in the North, and there he could compete against white players with less controversy.

In 1959, a year after Althea Gibson won both Wimbledon and the U.S. National Championships, Arthur Ashe entered his first U.S. Nationals. He lost to Australian tennis great Rod Laver in the first round. But he had taken the first steps of his tennis career.

In 1961, Ashe went west to UCLA, just as he had said he would. He followed his own path in other ways. While many athletes majored in physical education or other sports-related fields, Ashe studied business.

In 1963, he received a great honor. He became the first African-American to be named to the U.S. Davis Cup squad. The Davis Cup is an international tennis tournament in which teams of players from different countries compete against each other. When Arthur Ashe retired in 1978, his 27 Davis Cup wins were a record.

BEING NAMED TO THE U.S. DAVIS CUP TEAM IN 1963 WAS A GREAT TRIBUTE TO ARTHUR ASHE, WHO HITS A RETURN ON THE COURTS AT UCLA AFTER LEARNING THE NEWS.

Meanwhile, in his junior year at UCLA, Ashe became the first black to win the National Collegiate Athletic Association (NCAA) singles championship. He also led UCLA's squad to the NCAA team title. In 1966, he graduated with a degree in business administration.

The **civil rights movement** blossomed as Ashe was breaking down barriers in tennis. For years, attempts to end segregation were met with excuses, threats, or violence. Finally, by the mid-1960s, African-Americans had begun to gain civil rights. They could vote and go to white schools. Racist laws were being **repealed.**

Ashe saw a sign of change up close. In 1966, he returned to Richmond to play a tournament at Byrd Park. Five years earlier, park officials had thrown him out for trying to play tennis with whites. Now the same park had set up a special tournament to show him off.

This didn't mean that **prejudice** had disappeared. The Dallas Country Club refused to let Ashe play a Davis Cup match there because of his race. Later, the club closed down its annual tournament rather than include African-Americans. Other country clubs allowed blacks to play on their courts only in tournaments. Ashe was asked why he played in places where he would not be admitted as a member. "I don't like it at all," he said, "but I'm **resigned** to the fact that if I'm to play tennis, I have to play at these clubs because that's where tennis is. But not forever, I hope. I hope I see changes."

ARTHUR ASHE, HERE IN A 1965 DAVIS CUP MATCH, FACED MUCH PREJUDICE. ON THE COURT, HOWEVER, HE CONCENTRATED FULLY ON THE GAME.

At the same time, Ashe's tennis game improved. After joining the U.S. Army in 1966, he was allowed to keep playing as long as he remained an **amateur.** That meant he couldn't make money, but he got to play against top players in tournaments and in the Davis Cup. He perfected his booming serves, polished his footwork, and learned to rush the net and rattle opponents. Yet nothing seemed to bother him. "It was like playing a ghost out there," said legendary tennis coach Nick Bollettieri.

In 1968, Ashe thrilled fans at the U.S. amateur tournament with his style and intelligence. A breakthrough came later that year. Like so much else in the world, tennis was changing. The U.S. National Championships became the U.S. Open, and for the first time, the competition was open to both amateurs and **professionals.**

ASHE PLAYED TOM OKKER AS AN AMATEUR IN THE 1968 U.S. OPEN.

Ashe entered this tournament in the top five. The professional players were considered favorites. When the final was played, however, it was Arthur Ashe against Dutch pro Tom Okker. Ashe served 26 **aces** and triumphed in a close five-set match. No African-American man had ever won such a major tournament.

Of course, Ashe could not accept any prize money. Okker took home $14,000. But Ashe had won something greater. He had made history. His victory came without any issues over race.

IN 1968, ASHE BECAME THE FIRST BLACK MAN TO WIN THE U.S. OPEN. NEXT TO ASHE IS HIS FATHER, WHO FIGHTS TEARS AFTER HIS SON'S HISTORIC VICTORY.

Years later, Ashe quoted a prayer in his book *Days of Grace:* "Lord, make us not great but busy." As one of the world's most famous tennis players, Arthur Ashe could have stayed busy playing tennis, but he wanted to do more.

In 1969, he toured Asia for the U.S. State Department. On the trip, he led tennis clinics for children. In Vietnam, he played tennis to entertain U.S. soldiers and officers. That same year, his Davis Cup team defeated mighty Australia.

ASHE WORKED FOR THE U.S. STATE DEPARTMENT TOURING ASIA. HERE HE PLAYS IN A DEMONSTRATION TOURNAMENT IN VIETNAM.

Ashe had his first brush with controversy in March 1969. He gave a speech on civil rights at a church in Washington, D.C. Army officers, however, did not want soldiers speaking out on issues, and they ordered him not to make any more speeches.

THE U.S. DAVIS CUP TEAM DEFEATED AUSTRALIA IN 1968. ARTHUR ASHE AND TWO OTHER TEAM MEMBERS PROUDLY DISPLAY THE HONORED SYMBOL OF THE TENNIS WORLD'S GREATEST ACCOMPLISHMENT.

IN THE 1960s, ACTIVISTS MARCHED FOR CIVIL RIGHTS. ASHE FELT SOME GUILT FOR NOT BEING ONE OF THEM.

When he left the army, Ashe was free to fight for civil rights. Often he argued with African-American leaders Andrew Young and Jesse Jackson. Ashe preferred his own calm and modest approach. Years later, he admitted feeling some guilt for playing tennis while others sacrificed to end segregation. "There were times," he said, "when I felt a burning sense of shame that I was not with other blacks—and whites—standing up to the fire hoses and the police dogs, the [police officers' clubs], bullets, and bombs."

Despite his doubts, Ashe continued playing the Davis Cup and taking U.S. State Department tours of Vietnam and Africa. In 1972, he helped found a union of tennis players called the Association of Tennis Professionals (ATP). Ashe also spoke on issues concerning African-Americans. Yet he felt the urge to aim even higher. Arthur Ashe wanted to serve humanity. That desire would bring him more controversy than ever.

IN 1972, ASHE HELPED FOUND THE ASSOCIATION OF TENNIS PROFESSIONALS (ATP).

ASHE OFTEN SPOKE OUT AGAINST APARTHEID. IN 1970, HE ASKED A UNITED NATIONS SPECIAL COMMITTEE TO BAR SOUTH AFRICA FROM THE INTERNATIONAL LAWN TENNIS FEDERATION AND DAVIS CUP COMPETITION.

Great but Busy

In the early 1970s, not many Americans paid attention to the Republic of South Africa or its system of **apartheid.** Apartheid divided South Africa's society. On one side were whites. On the other stood Africans, "coloreds" (people of mixed race), and Indians. South Africa reminded Ashe of Richmond. He read about the country and talked to white South Africans on the tennis tour. However, he was able to learn only so much that way.

In 1973, Ashe was allowed to play in the South African Open. South Africa's government agreed to let him go where he wanted and do what he wanted. In return, he promised not to talk about apartheid during his visit.

APARTHEID IN SOUTH AFRICA MEANT GREAT POVERTY FOR BLACK AFRICANS.

People immediately criticized Ashe's decision to play. To many, playing in South Africa seemed to be a favor to the apartheid government, which often hosted sporting events in an effort to show its society in a positive light. Ashe felt it was the only way to get into the country. "I know they're using me," he said, "but I'm using them, too."

Ashe wanted to learn. He also wanted black South Africans to see a black man playing against white players to show that blacks were equal in sports and should be treated as equals in all other ways. At his request, the tennis tournament got rid of segregated seating during his matches. They also allowed 10 nonwhite South Africans to play in the tournament.

On the court, he proved his point by beating two white South African players and getting to the singles championship. He lost, but he won the doubles trophy with Tom Okker. Black fans in the audience watched with tears in their eyes. Soon they were calling him Sipho—the **Zulu** word for "gift."

Off the court, he studied life under apartheid. He played tennis in Soweto, a poor black township. About 2,000 people watched him. They climbed on top of billboards or railroad tracks to see him. "Apartheid pauses for you, Arthur," one black man told him.

Others disagreed. Don Mattera, a colored poet banned from publishing his work, tried to convince Ashe that he had been wrong to come. Ashe explained his reasons. Days later, as Ashe prepared to go home, someone handed him a rolled-up newspaper. Inside was a poem by Mattera in which he expressed respect for Ashe.

DURING HIS VISIT TO SOUTH AFRICA IN 1973, ASHE WENT TO THE BLACK TOWN-SHIP OF SOWETO. THE TENNIS LEGEND WAS SURROUNDED BY YOUNG PEOPLE.

A she blasted the South African government the moment he returned to the United States. For the rest of his life, he campaigned against apartheid. Meanwhile, Ashe continued to play excellent tennis.

In 1975, Ashe shocked everyone by winning the biggest tournament of all—Wimbledon. Jimmy Connors, the defending champion, was considered unbeatable. A thinker as always, Ashe had prepared by studying his opponent's weaknesses. He avoided Connors's strong backhand. He hit his shots low, a trick he had learned in Richmond. He kept calm when Connors won the third set in a best-of-five-sets match. After winning the fourth set, Ashe raised a fist in the air. He had become the first black Wimbledon men's champion. He didn't know it, but Wimbledon would be his last major title.

ARTHUR ASHE HOLDS UP HIS WIMBLEDON TROPHY CUP AFTER DEFEATING FELLOW AMERICAN JIMMY CONNORS IN 1975.

In 1977, Arthur Ashe married Jeanne Moutoussamy, a professional photographer. Ashe attended the wedding on crutches after foot surgery. His old friend Andrew Young, then the U.S. ambassador to the United Nations, performed the ceremony. Unfortunately, the crutches were a symbol of Ashe's future health.

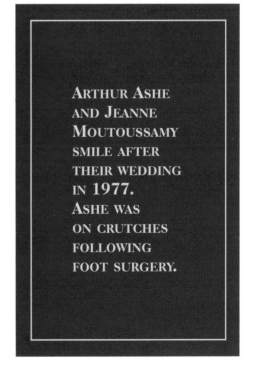

ARTHUR ASHE AND JEANNE MOUTOUSSAMY SMILE AFTER THEIR WEDDING IN 1977. ASHE WAS ON CRUTCHES FOLLOWING FOOT SURGERY.

One night in 1979, Ashe woke up with chest pains. After tests, the doctors told him all four valves in his heart were blocked.

Heart disease ran in Ashe's family. However, Ashe was young and in great shape. He hoped that surgery would allow him to play tennis again. After another problem with his heart during training, though, he knew his career was over.

Ashe finished his playing career in 1980 with 33 singles titles and 18 doubles titles. What had the prayer said? "Lord, make us not great but busy." He had been great. Now, with his playing career over, Ashe faced the challenge of staying busy.

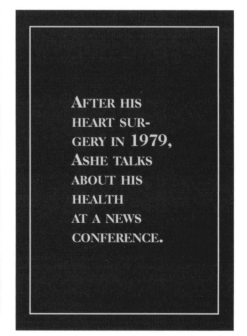

AFTER HIS HEART SURGERY IN 1979, ASHE TALKS ABOUT HIS HEALTH AT A NEWS CONFERENCE.

A Messenger

A she knew he needed some kind of bridge to connect his playing career and the rest of his life. He decided that bridge would be teaching tennis. Even as a player, Ashe had offered support and advice to others. Rodney Harmon, an African-American player from Richmond, later earned a place on the professional tour. So did Yannick Noah, a talented teenager from Cameroon whom Ashe had met in Africa. Ashe also held clinics for children and taught at a Florida country club.

AFTER RETIRING FROM PROFESSIONAL TENNIS, ASHE WORKED WITH MANY YOUNG BLACK PLAYERS.

In 1980, Arthur Ashe got the opportunity of a lifetime. He was asked to be the coach, or captain, of the U.S. Davis Cup team. In his five years as captain, the United States won in 1981 and in 1982. He finished with a 13–3 record. During the Davis Cup years, Ashe suffered another heart attack. He had surgery again. Soon he complained he was tired and weak. Doctors gave him fresh blood—a process called a transfusion—and he felt better.

Ashe added the American Heart Association to his list of causes. Ashe liked to wear a T-shirt that said Citizen of the World. When he stepped down as the Davis Cup captain in 1985, "Citizen of the World" became his full-time job.

By 1985, many Americans were marching against apartheid. Ashe planned to march in Washington, D.C., where he knew he would be arrested. That bothered him. He had spent his life being a role model. Yet, he remembered when he could not play tennis in all-white tournaments. He remembered the years after that, when people of all colors were hurt or killed fighting for civil rights. He had to take a stand.

On January 11, 1985, he was arrested during a protest. "Marching in a protest is a liberating experience," he said. He also gave speeches and cofounded a group called Artists and Athletes Against Apartheid. He would see the end of apartheid, but first a new challenge and a new cause entered his life.

In 1988, Ashe went to see his doctor about numbness in his hand. His doctor said he needed brain surgery. When he had blood tests done before the operation, Ashe was shocked to find out he had human immunodeficiency virus, or HIV, the virus that can lead to AIDS.

MUSIC PRODUCER QUINCY JONES, SOUTH AFRICAN POLITICAL LEADER NELSON MANDELA, CIVIL RIGHTS ACTIVIST RANDALL ROBINSON SIT (LEFT TO RIGHT) WITH ASHE AT A MEDIA CONFERENCE IN 1991.

orse news was to come. During surgery, doctors discovered that Ashe had AIDS. Ashe believed he got HIV from the blood he had received after his second heart operation. Unfortunately, that blood turned out to be from someone with HIV. Ashe was not the only patient to have this happen. More than 10,000 people got AIDS from transfusions before scientists found a way to test for infected blood.

Ashe and his wife decided to keep the news from all but a few friends. Then Ashe did what he always did—he learned everything possible. He called it being a professional patient, but he did not give up. "Despair is a state of mind to which I refuse to surrender," he said.

Though his medicine made him weak, he started a group to help college athletes after graduation. He also became interested in the history of African-American athletes. When he saw that their stories had never been told, he hired a staff and wrote them himself. His book, *A Hard Road to Glory,* published in 1988, is still considered one of the most important works on the subject. When it was turned into a television special, Ashe wrote the script.

Finally, as the 1980s ended, apartheid crumbled. Ashe met South Africa's most famous prisoner, Nelson Mandela, who later served as president of the country. The two men became friends. Mandela invited Ashe to South Africa in 1991 to see how it had changed. Ashe met with him and with Don Mattera, the poet he had argued with in 1973.

Meanwhile, Ashe's secret was in danger. A newspaper reporter asked Ashe if he had AIDS. Unwilling to lie, Ashe refused to answer, but he knew that the news would soon leak out. He wanted people to hear it from him, not the newspapers. With his wife and friends at his side, he announced to the world that he had AIDS.

Right away, he started a group dedicated to wiping out AIDS. He recruited celebrities and tennis players to raise money for it. The U.S. Open hosted Arthur Ashe AIDS Day. Ashe called it "one of the brightest days . . . of my life."

Though he knew he was running out of time, he started a book about his life after tennis called *Days of Grace.* In 1992, he asked the United Nations to spend more money on AIDS around the world. He was arrested again, this time for pro-testing the government's poor treatment of Haitian **refugees.** *Sports Illustrated* named him its Sportsman of the Year for his work helping others.

ON APRIL 8, 1992, ASHE TOLD THE WORLD HE HAD AIDS. HIS WIFE STOOD BY HIS SIDE AT THE EMOTIONAL PRESS CONFERENCE.

T hough ill, Arthur Ashe refused to complain, which surprised many. "I'm not a victim," he liked to say. "I'm a messenger." "He never complained about his fate," said Stan Smith, a former tennis player and an old friend. "This attitude goes back to when he wasn't allowed to play in a club, or he wasn't able to go into a particular tournament, or he wasn't able to go into their clubhouse."

Ashe began February 1993 with plans for a Valentine's Day dance for himself, his daughter Camera, and friends. He never made it. He died on February 6.

ASHE HOLDS CAMERA, HIS FIVE-YEAR-OLD DAUGHTER, AT A TENNIS BENEFIT FOR AIDS IN 1992. HE DIED THE NEXT YEAR, AT THE AGE OF 49.

Arthur Ashe was buried in his hometown of Richmond, Virginia. Some 6,000 people passed by his casket as it lay in the governor's mansion. Three years later, the city built a statue of Ashe on its famous Monument Avenue. He was the first African-American to be honored in this way. Since his death, the organizations Ashe started or worked with have helped countless people—from kids picking up a tennis racket for the first time to those with AIDS or heart disease. A quote from Arthur Ashe engraved at the National Tennis Center in Flushing Meadows, New York, sums up his life: "From what we get, we make a living; what we give, however, makes a life."

THE ARTHUR ASHE STADIUM WAS NAMED AFTER THE TENNIS LEGEND IN 1997.

Timeline

1943	Arthur Robert Ashe Jr. is born on July 10 to Arthur Robert Ashe Sr. and Mattie Cordell Cunningham Ashe in Richmond, Virginia.
1953	Ashe spends the first of nine summers with his coach, Dr. Robert Walter Johnson.
1959	Ashe plays for the first time in the U.S. National Championships (later the U.S. Open), losing to Australian star Rod Laver.
1961	Ashe enrolls at University of California at Los Angeles (UCLA).
1963	Ashe joins the U.S. Davis Cup squad, becoming the first African-American member of the team.
1965	Ashe wins the NCAA singles championship. He also leads UCLA's tennis squad to the NCAA team title.
1966	Ashe graduates from UCLA with a degree in business administration. Later that year, he joins the U.S. Army.
1968	Ashe wins the U.S. Amateur tournament and the first U.S. Open Championships.
1969	On a trip for the U.S. State Department, Ashe visits Vietnam and plays tennis to entertain the soldiers and officers. The same year, he cofounds the National Junior Tennis League (NJTL), a program to teach the game to inner-city children.
1970	Ashe wins the Australian Open.
1972	Ashe helps found a union of tennis players called the Association of Tennis Professionals.
1973	Ashe plays in the South African Open. He tours the country to learn about apartheid.

1975	Ashe defeats Jimmy Connors in the Wimbledon singles final and becomes the first black man to win the world's most celebrated tennis tournament.
1977	Ashe marries Jeanne Moutoussamy in a ceremony performed by Ashe's friend Andrew Young, the U.S. ambassador to the United Nations.
1978	Ashe plays the last of his 32 Davis Cup matches. He retires from Davis Cup with 27 victories, a record at the time.
1979	Ashe undergoes a major heart operation.
1980	After retiring from playing tennis, Ashe becomes captain of the U.S. Davis Cup team.
1981	As captain, Ashe leads the U.S. Davis Cup team to victory. (They win again in 1982.)
1983	After a second heart attack, Ashe undergoes surgery again.
1985	Ashe is arrested at an antiapartheid demonstration in Washington, D.C. In the summer, he is named to the International Tennis Hall of Fame. Later that year, he steps down as the Davis Cup captain.
1988	Ashe undergoes brain surgery and finds out he has AIDS. He publishes *A Hard Road to Glory: A History of the African-American Athlete*.
1992	Ashe is arrested for protesting the government's poor treatment of Haitian refugees. He addresses the United Nations to argue for more money for AIDS research and treatment. *Sports Illustrated* names Ashe Sportsman of the Year.
1993	Ashe dies on February 6 of pneumonia complicated by AIDS. He is buried in Richmond, Virginia.
1997	The main U.S. Open stadium is named after Ashe. It is the largest tennis stadium in the world.

Glossary

aces (AY-sez)
Aces are tennis serves that the other player fails to hit. Ashe served 26 aces in the final of the 1968 U.S. Open.

activist (AK-tih-vist)
An activist is someone who takes direct action for a particular cause. Ashe was an activist in many causes.

amateur (AM-uh-chur)
An amateur is someone who participates in a sport for fun rather than money. When Ashe was an amateur, he was not allowed to earn money for playing tennis.

apartheid (uh-PART-hite)
Apartheid is a political system in which whites discriminate against nonwhites. It usually refers to the former government of the Republic of South Africa. In 1973, Ashe went to South Africa to play tennis and see apartheid for himself.

**civil rights movement
(SIV-il rites MOOV-muhnt)**
The civil rights movement took place in the 1950s and 1960s in the United States. Blacks and whites joined together to gain equal laws and equal rights for African-Americans. Ashe came of age during the civil rights movement.

prejudice (PREJ-uh-diss)
Prejudice is a fixed or unfair opinion about someone based on his or her race or religion. As a black tennis player, Ashe faced much prejudice.

professionals (pruh-FESH-uh-nuhlz)
Professionals make money for doing something others do for pleasure. In 1972, Ashe helped found a union of tennis professionals.

refugees (ref-yuh-JEEZ)
Refugees are people who are forced from their homes because of war, natural disaster, or poor treatment. In 1992, Ashe was arrested for protesting the government's poor treatment of Haitian refugees.

repealed (ree-PEELD)
To repeal something is to do away with it. Racist laws in the United States were being repealed by the mid-1960s.

resigned (ree-ZINED)
To be resigned means to accept what comes without complaining. Before civil rights laws changed, Ashe said he was resigned to a certain amount of prejudice at tennis clubs.

segregated (SEH-greh-GAY-tid)
Segregated means organized to keep whites and blacks apart by maintaining separate public facilities. When Ashe was a child in Richmond, Virginia, many public places were segregated.

Zulu (ZOO-loo)
The Zulu are one of the Bantu-speaking peoples of southern Africa and one of the biggest groups in the Republic of South Africa. *Zulu* also refers to their language. Zulu people called Ashe their word for "gift," which is *Sipho*.

Index

Further Information

Books

Lazo, Caroline Evensen. *Arthur Ashe.* Minneapolis: Lerner, 1999.

Martin, Marvin. *Arthur Ashe: Of Tennis & the Human Spirit.* Danbury, Conn.: Franklin Watts, 1998.

Moutoussamy-Ashe, Jeanne (photography and text). *Daddy and Me: A Photo Story of Arthur Ashe and His Daughter.* New York: Knopf, 1993.

Wright, David K. *Arthur Ashe: Breaking the Color Barrier in Tennis.* Springfield, N.J.: Enslow, 1996.

Web Sites

Visit our homepage for lots of links about Arthur Ashe:

http://www.childsworld.com/links.html

Note to Parents, Teachers, and Librarians:
We routinely verify our Web links to make sure they're safe,
active sites—so encourage your readers to check them out!

About the Author

Kevin Cunningham is an author and travel writer. He studied journalism and history at the University of Illinois at Urbana. As a student, he became interested in African-American culture through studies of the civil rights movement, Harlem Renaissance, and black music. His other books include *The Canadian Americans* and *Condoleezza Rice: Educator and Presidential Adviser.* He lives in Chicago.